In Youth With A Mission (YWAM) we live by faith. This means trusting the Lord for His provision where He calls us. This often involves inviting others to partner with this calling through their financial support. This book is one of the good books that helps people get started in order to find financial partners for missionary service. God's ways of provision however are so much greater they can't all be captured in one book, so I leave you with a word of encouragement- Wherever God is calling you, be faithful in doing the possible and He will do the impossible.

Loren Cunningham, Founder, YWAM

Having tried to help many raise support over the years I know a good resource when I see one. This book is practical, gives a clear process and strong on relationships and communication.

Laurence Singlehurst
Former YWAM England Director, Speaker and Author, Chairman of
Westminster Theological Centre

This is a great little book with some basic methodology for support raising. It covers basic budgeting, setting targets and strategy, and keeping good records of your current and potential supporters. All things we would highly recommend.

OSCAR.org.uk

There are many different biblical and historical models of financing the church and missionary work. Some books go really deep into theory and talking about lofty ideas, this is not one of them. Instead, you have 12 short and to the point chapters with actionable steps that will help you raise your support.

Chris Wilson, ChurchMag

I've been a missionary for the past 29 years. I've read different books on fundraising but I really liked Chris Staplehurst's book about these easy steps. I think it's very simple. My wife and I have already applied these steps and we saw some breakthroughs. I highly recommend it for missionaries and others that are in a place where they need to connect with others to do fundraising for themselves or for projects they are involved in.

Stefaan Hugo
YWAM Southern Africa and Europe

My wife and I have been living the "relationship-based support" lifestyle for over 12 years now, working with Youth With A Mission. Support raising is never easy, but the suggestions in this little book are so practical that they look like they'll take the stress right out of that part of the job. I love Chris Staplehurst's focus on relationship with supporters. That really is the heart of the matter.

Rick Joyce, YWAM England

Knowing where to begin is often the barrier, but this book takes you on a whistlestop tour of support raising. Chris gives the what, how, and validation of speaking with others to share in a ministry project. He reminds us that there really are people out there who also believe that the same things are important and that they are worth investing in. The bottom line comes down to relationships and communication, but the ideas he presents will spark more ideas into specific situations and fuel courage in the way forward.

Linda Leage, YWAM England

12 EASY ACTIONS
FOR RAISING SUPPORT

An Introductory Practical
Guide For Missionaries

Chris Staplehurst

CONTENTS

Introduction

This book was initially created to help a married couple with four children in missions. Like most missionaries, they had lots of things going on, including meeting their financial needs. The book is designed for those who need a basic framework to organize their financial support and communicate with supporters.

For over three years I relied on relationship-based support, serving with Youth With A Mission (YWAM). Now I find myself on the other side of the fence, being a ministry partner and financial supporter. In more recent times, I have worked in communication roles in London (UK) and have learnt some principles in regard to financial support, which I feel are applicable to missionaries.

It's generally understood at the moment that missionaries do not like asking for financial support. In addition to this prospect, there is uncertainty on whether it is Biblical to ask for finances. It's a taboo subject amongst missionaries and missionary communities, which I hope will change.

Biblically, it can be suggested that there are various ways on the giving and receiving of finances for ministry. With Jesus, money was not a taboo subject. He talked about it, a lot. Jesus had financial supporters who believed in him and his ministry (e.g. Luke 8:1-3). On his mission's trips, the apostle Paul shared financial needs as well (e.g. 2 Corinthians, chapters 8 and 9). The Levi tribe received tithes from the other 11 tribes in their dedicated service to the tabernacle (Numbers 1:50 and 18:1-24).

Some well-known missionaries such as George Müller and Hudson Taylor explicitly did not ask for finances. However, the accounting of their ministries would have been publicly known to the government and to those who were aware of the ministry and were interested in financially supporting their ministries.

Raising support comes down to your relationship with God and how God is leading you to conduct your finances. If through prayer and direction God is leading you to not ask for financial support, this book may still be of interest for you, as it discusses ways of how to nurture your relationships and communicate effectively with ministry partners and financial supporters. Whichever direction you are being led with your ministry finances, there are people out there who would like to financially support missionaries to further the Kingdom, and they are closer than you think!

EASY ACTION

#1

Current
Financial Support

First of all, let's identify who is supporting you right now. Following the example below start filling in your current financial supporters using the template on the next page (or you can open up a spreadsheet or grab a piece of paper).

For one-off donations that occur each year or so, divide the sum by 12 to show an approximate monthly amount given. Highlight the one-off supporters (e.g. David Wilson (one-off)), as they could become monthly supporters in the future to ask.

Date _____ Supporter No.	Name of Supporter	Monthly Giving
1	Home Church	500
2	Trinity Church	400
3	Ben Baden	200
4	Katie Smith	100
5	Dora Bell	100
6	Jeff's Church - HTLC	75
7	Fran and David	50
8	James and Jenny Hill	50
9	Andy and Alice Reynolds	50
10	Corey Smith (one-off)	25
...	...	...
...	...	...
	Total Support	_____

Current Financial Supporters

Date _____ Supporter No.	Name of Supporter	Monthly Giving
1		
2		
3		
4		
5		
6		
7		
8		
9		
10		
11		
12		
13		
14		
15		
16		
17		
18		
19		
20		
21		
22		
23		
24		
25		
	Total Support	_____

"For all the animals of the forest are mine, and I own the cattle on a thousand hills."

Psalms 50:10

EASY ACTION

#2

Determine
The Need

We will now explore all your needs to find out how much financially you require for your ministry. List absolutely every desired need currently and in the near future. Viewing your bank statement is a good way to find where money is spent. For annual expenses divide by 12 to get the monthly amount. Here are examples of expenses below. Some will be monthly regular costs and less frequent which should also be included.

	Expense Type
1	Food / Household Needs
2	House: Rent / Deposit / Water / Gas / Electric / Internet
3	Tithing
4	Mobile Phone
5	Gym/Leisure Activities/Kids Clubs
6	Pension
7	Car (Fuel, Insurance, Tax, Maintenance)
8	Medical (e.g. Dentist, Doctor, Medication)
9	Personal Treats (sports tickets, spa)
10	Couple Time / Coffee / Cinema
11	Holidays
12	Clothing
13	Ministry & Missions
14	Clubs / Training Courses
15	Emergency Savings (e.g. flight back home)
16	Regular Savings
17	Birthday Presents / Christmas Presents
18	Children's School Expenses
19	Child Care/Maintenance
20	Miscellaneous

Current Financial Needs

To discover your current financial needs run through the examples on the previous page and complete the table below. Alternatively, create the table and write up the list on a spreadsheet. Add them up at the bottom to get you total financial needs.

Date_____	Expense Type	Cost per Month
1		
2		
3		
4		
5		
6		
7		
8		
9		
10		
11		
12		
13		
14		
15		
16		
17		
18		
19		
20		
	Total Expenses	_____

"And God is able to bless you abundantly, so that in all things at all times, having all that you need, you will abound in every good work."

2 Corinthians 9:8

EASY ACTION

ACTION

#3

The Current
Position

Total Support

(Easy Action #1, p5)

–

Total Expenses

(Easy Action #2, p9)

= The Current Position

This will be quick. Now, from what you have found out from *Easy Action #1* and *#2* put the figures together to discover what the current position is in regards to your finances.

Date: _____

Total Support = _____

(*Easy Action # 1, p5*)

Total Expenses = _____

(*Easy Action # 2, p9*)

Current Position = _____

Whatever the current financial situation is, know that God is in control. Do not be alarmed if a deficit seems large in number. A spirit of poverty or being poor as an expectation can cause thoughts about not deserving things like new clothes for yourself and your family, a new car or a house.

If there is a surplus, double check that all needs have been added (check anyway). Think and pray about using your surplus to give to others (for example, supporting other missionaries in building the Kingdom of God). Now that we know where things stand, let's look at explore some ways with how to maintain and build your ministry relationships and your financial support.

"But seek ye first the kingdom of God, and his righteousness; and all these things shall be added unto you"

Matthew 6:33

EASY
ACTION

#4

Asking Supporters
For An Increase

Using the *List of Supporters* started in *Easy Action #1*, add these two columns onto your spreadsheet, or you can use the template on the next page.

	Name of Supporter	Monthly Giving	Suggested Increase	Date Last Asked for Finance
1	Home Church	500	-	Oct 2019
2	Trinity Church	400	-	Oct 2019
3	Ben Baden	200	-	Jan 2019
4	Katie Smith	100	10	Jun 2018
5	Dora Bell	100	20	Apr 2019
6	Jeff's Church	75	-	Jan 2020
7	Fran and David	50	10	May 2019
8	James and Jenny Hill	50	10	Mar 2019
	Total Support	————	————	

Current Financial Supporters That I Could Ask
(see page 5)

	Name of Supporter	Monthly Giving	Suggested Increase	Date Last Asked for Finance
1				
2				
3				
4				
5				
6				
7				
8				
9				
10				
11				
12				
13				
14				
15				
	Total Support	————	————	

In the next column add the date when you last personally asked for an increase in finances. Other columns you could add include:

Record How Your Supporters Joined

For an extra column record how your supporters became your supporters. For example, they might have joined due to a home group meeting or church presentation. There may be a trend that is evident with how, or when, or why your supporters decide to join. This may help you communicate and generate more supporters in the future.

Record When Your Supporters Respond

Note the answer, reason and date when a supporter has responded. Did they say yes, no or maybe? It's very important to record these answers, as this will determine how and when you communicate with them in the future. For example, a supporter might have just finished paying off a holiday and say something on the lines of:

> *"Hi Chris, Thanks for your message and newsletter earlier this month. If you had asked a month ago I would've said no, but now things are looking better financially I'll be happy to increase my support. God bless!"*

Another example could be that the supporter can't give to you financially right now but that you should ask them again in 3 months.

  People who tithe to other ministries may have had a change in circumstances and became aware of your ministry, showed an interest and subsequently wanted to join. In this case the supporter is a warm lead and should be followed up at the appointed time. Get in touch with them to reconnect. Build back the relationship if needed and don't try to force the issue. Share life together and in doing so there will be a time to ask if they would like to sign up to the newsletter, or be kept in touch with your ministry and then asking for financial partnership.

In this section let's find how to ask for an increase in financial support from your current supporters. Some of this section will also apply when asking people to be new supporters as well.

*When was the last time you asked
for an increase in financial support?*

If this is a new idea to you do not fret. It should be reasonable to request an increase in support at least every 1 or 2 years. Your supporters know things change in life, like a new addition to the family or a health situation for example. Share your financial needs with them. Always remember that these supporters are your partners in the ministry and want to see it grow and develop, and with that financial needs may increase as well.

It is best to just simply be honest with the reason you're asking for an increase in support. If they believe in what you are doing then trust that God is leading you both in his plans and purposes. Do not be afraid of them leaving when asking for an increase. If they do leave on the prompting of you asking there's no harm in questioning why. This may provide some valuable insight for your ministry to learn from. For example, if you repeatedly contact a supporter solely asking for money, that might cause a negative response. Hopefully, as you read through this book you'll find more to share about with your supporters than just issues around money.

Asking supporters if they might need to decrease their support might be suitable at times, especially if circumstances have changed such as a change of job. Approaching someone to ask for finance all depends on the nature of the person and the relationship you have with them. Some supporters will wish to support you and may not be in contact that often.

Others however may wish to know what's happening on a more frequent basis.

Ask at suitable times in the week, month or year when the supporter will be more available to respond. Most people are working Monday to Friday and have the weekend to rest and do other activities. Contacting supporters on a Saturday morning provides ample time over the weekend for a supporter or potential supporter to read your message, make a decision and act upon the decision made. Everyone has different schedules however, so I would suggest finding out what the schedule is of someone you are messaging is.

Generally, there are times of the year when money is likely to be tighter, such as after Christmas (especially if supporters have a family to provide for) and so be aware of the times of year that might more suitable to get in touch. It's also important to ask in the right way too as you should look to be honest and positive on your request knowing that you, your ministry and partnership will benefit from this request being actioned. Let's look at this request,

> *"Would you consider adding $10 on to*
> *your monthly support?"*

This statement is asking in a good manner and tone. Using the word *'consider'* is giving the supporter a chance to think about the question. *'Adding $10'* focuses on the amount you are asking for, which is a clearer message of the intended change, rather than mentioning the total level of support that someone is giving plus an adding the increase. Make it clear what you are asking for.

Finding when and how to ask for support makes the process more effective as the intention behind it is good. For a supporter or potential supporter, it shows that you care and are willing to make the effort to adapt your schedule with theirs. It is about your ministry and thriving in it and supporters want that, as it is their ministry too. As both parties confidently work together this will only boost the ministry and everyone involved. *Teamwork makes the dream work.*

"The LORD is my shepherd, I lack nothing."

Psalms 23:1

EASY
ACTION

#5

Warm Potential Supporters

Warm and *Cold* are classification terms in business communications to signify a level of contact with you and someone else. *Warm Potential Supporters* refers to people you have spoken to about the ministry and have indicated that they might possibly be interested in supporting you if you were to ask them.

Date 05/04/20	Name of Supporter	Suggested Monthly Giving
1	Kay and Steve	50
2	Jeff Smith	50
3	Kylie's Uncle	20
4	Paula Jones	10
5	Matt's Church	100
6	Fran Davids (one-off)	10 *(until April 2021)*
7	Brendan	*Amount not specified yet but he said he will support*
...	...	...
...	...	...
	Warm Potential Supporters Support	————

Enter in every person you can think of that has shown a desire to become a financial supporter. There could be a lot more *Warm Potential Supporters* if we dig a little more. List also every contact that is on your email list that is reading your emails (or just on your list) but does not financially support you. There are two pages to fill here to get started.

Warm Potential Supporters *(List 1)*

Date _____	Name of Supporter	Suggested Monthly Giving
1		
2		
3		
4		
5		
6		
7		
8		
9		
10		
11		
12		
13		
14		
15		

Warm Potential Supporters *(List 2)*

Date _____	Name of Supporter	Suggested Monthly Giving
16		
17		
18		
19		
20		
21		
22		
23		
24		
25		
26		
27		
28		
29		
30		
	Total Warm Potential Support	

"Do not be anxious about anything, but in every situation, by prayer and petition, with thanksgiving, present your requests to God."

Philippians 4:6

EASY
ACTION

#6

Cold Potential
Supporters

Cold Potential Supporters refers to people you haven't spoken to about the ministry, but think that they might be interested in supporting you if you were to ask them.

Date 12/08/20	Name of Potential Supporter	Suggested Monthly Giving
1	Rachel Barton	10
2	Mark Boothe	30
3	Maisie Jones	25
4	Pete Smith	20
5	Dwayne Henderson	100
6	Dean Harding (one-off)	10
7	TBC – Kylie's church (one-off)	50
	Cold Potential Support	**245**

Most people tend to make assumptions about what other people may think without asking them. Don't rely on your assumptions. They may not be accurate, negative and based on thoughts like *'They won't support me'*. Politely ask the person to consider being a financial supporter and you will either get yes, no or maybe and you'll know where you stand rather than relying on assumptions.

Think of people who might pray for you regularly, or people who are associated with your ministry work or generally interested in how you are doing. They might be on your email list but are not financially supporting you.

Ask supporters if they know people that might be interested could be a good idea. Take the time to make an exhaustive list. Test your assumptions and you will be surprised. Once again, there are two pages to help create these lists.

Cold Potential Supporters *(List 1)*

Date _____	Name of Supporter	Suggested Monthly Giving
1		
2		
3		
4		
5		
6		
7		
8		
9		
10		
11		
12		
13		
14		
15		

Cold Potential Supporters *(List 2)*

Date _____	Name of Supporter	Suggested Monthly Giving
16		
17		
18		
19		
20		
21		
22		
23		
24		
25		
26		
27		
28		
29		
30		
	Total Cold Potential Support	

"Consider the ravens: The do not sow or reap, they no storeroom or barn; yet God feeds them. And how much more valuable you are than birds!"

Luke 12:24

EASY ACTION
#7

Discover Your Potential Support

This shouldn't take long. It's quick and easy and will help you visualise where your finances are currently. Taking your previous calculations, enter the new figures here to see the new potential (NEW TOTAL) support.

Total Support = _____

(Easy Action # 1, p5)

Total Expenses = _____

(Easy Action # 2, p9)

Current Position = _____

(Easy Action # 3, p13)

Total Support   _____

(Easy Action # 1, p5)

+

Total Suggested Increase   _____

(Easy Action # 4, p17)

+

Warm Potential Support   _____

(Easy Action # 5, p26)

+

Cold Potential Support   _____

(Easy Action # 6, p32)

NEW TOTAL   _____

Let's now look at the important area of how to communicate to these potential supporters.

*"...those who seek the LORD
lack no good thing."*

Psalm 34:10b

EASY
ACTION

#8

Find The Best Way
To Communicate

For every person you contact think about and note down what their preferred method of communication is. Fill in the table on the next page or add another column if you are building a spreadsheet. Here are some of the most common forms of communication.

- Email
- Phone Call
- Text Message
- Face-to-Face Meeting
- WhatsApp Message
- Video Chat
- Letter in the Post
- Presentation at Church/Home Group

Whatever communication is the supporters' preference, try your best to use it when communicating with them. If a person likes letters in the post then add some quality and love to the letters such as printed pictures.

Another key action, which we have mentioned previously in *Easy Action #4*, is to think when would be the best time to get in touch. Perhaps they work shifts? Do they have small children to look after? Are they going through a tough time? Think about how and when to communicate. It's important to be specific and to be kept up-to-date, as preferred methods can change.

If you don't get a response from the person keep in mind that they might not have seen the message. They might be busy with other priorities in their life. Don't be afraid to send it again or perhaps get in touch with the person through another form of communication until you get an answer.

For those of you that have created a spreadsheet for your supporters add a column and write down the best method of communication for all of your current and potential supporters.

Preferred Method of Communication

No.	Supporter Name	Communication Preference	Best Time/Day To Contact
1			
2			
3			
4			
5			
6			
7			
8			
9			
10			
11			
12			

No.	Supporter Name	Communication Preference	Best Time/Day To Contact
13			
14			
15			
16			
17			
18			
19			
20			
21			
22			
23			
24			
25			

"Consider the ravens: The do not sow or reap, they no storeroom or barn; yet God feeds them. And how much more valuable you are than birds!"

Luke 12:24

EASY
ACTION

#9

Spice Up
Your Emails

As technology continues to change the communications landscape, email has remained as an effective method of contact. With this in mind, it is important to make the best use of this tool for getting in touch with supporters.

If you are sending personalised newsletters to each of your supporters, that's great if you are doing that and have the time. However, if your newsletter is generic and you're still sending to each contact individually, you could save time and effort as well as gain useful insights by using a free email marketing service provider.

There are some brilliant providers out there that are free and friendly to use. The most popular email platform currently is Mailchimp. An email management service holds plenty of features, such as email templates, storage for images and supporters' email addresses. It also reveals which supporters are opening and clicking on the emails and also which ones are not. This is very useful to know in terms of making sure your communications gets through to all your supporters.

If somebody doesn't open your email after a few days, I would suggest sending the same email a week after the first email. If the person doesn't open the second email after a few days then look to get in touch through another method such as a phone call, WhatsApp message or text message.

There might be a small contingent who are quite happy to support you in your ministry and wish to not be informed of your ministry and its needs. They are most likely content with knowing they are funding you and your ministry. Most people however do want to hear from you. They do not just want to hear what your financial needs are however, they wish to partner with you and support you in different ways.

Try to schedule and write a range of emails that tell your supporters about you and your ministry. It will help keep your supporters' informed and engaged. Keep in mind that you are seeking to build relationships with people and partners in ministry.

Here are a few suggestions of types of emails to send out.

Regular emails

- Monthly newsletter
- Key dates (e.g. a supporter's birthday, Christmas.)
- Personal message from you
- Personal message from spouse, children
- Annual 'Thank You' message to supporters

One-off emails

- Asking for finances for a missions trip
- Asking for financial support to potential supporter
- Asking for an increase of financial support
- Special occasions (weddings, ministry milestone)
- Introduction to ministry to a new contact
- Financial report/summary
- Offer to visit supporter
- Offer to speak at supporter's church
- Invitation for supporters to visit
- Fundraising for another ministry
- Supporter leaving 'Thank You' message

A good idea to help plan and organise the communication with supporters is to get a wall calendar or diary. It's very easy to forget to contact supporters when you're in full-time ministry so you need to create reminders to help you stay on course to be consistent with your communication.

What Makes An Email Interesting And Engaging?

1) An Interesting Subject Line

News always appreciates having a great headline. What's your headline? An interesting subject line (or email title) grabs the reader's attention in a few words. Your supporters want to hear how you're doing. Encourage a reader's curiosity with an intriguing subject line that makes them want to open the email and find out more. Even if you think the content is boring, try and have some fun with *the mundane*. Add personalisation by using the supporter's first name in the subject line (you can add this on Mailchimp and most email management platforms). Adding an emoji is always interesting.

A rule of thumb is to think that if you are not interested with the email subject line then, chances are, your reader won't be either! Take a look at emails in your account from other organisations and people to glean some ideas. Sign up to receive newsletters from organisations you think might provide inspiration. Let's look specifically at newsletters as an example,

Subject lines for newsletters that you see might be:
1. January Newsletter
2. Frank's Newsletter
3. Jack and Rachel's latest news

Are these subject lines leaping off the page? Not really. They're quite dry, generic and they don't inform the reader anything specific to make it interesting.

Better subject lines for newsletters:
1. Tom's Recent Visit To Uganda
2. Chris, We're Starting A New Project In January
3. Meet Anna, Our New Volunteer!

2) A Story

Ministry stories: share the good stories; be concise. Add pictures with them if you can. If you have a website or private Facebook Group, use it to share the longer version of the story; ensure you have a good headline with a button (labelled for example 'Read More') to get your supporters to go to the website or web link.

3) Quality Images/Videos

- Especially good if you're smiling!
- The picture/video with a ministry related background
- People working with you or ones that you're ministering to (providing you have permission)

Videos are increasingly common now due to smartphones and increased access to the Internet. Create a YouTube account and link your video into your email for people to click on.

4) Quote/Testimony/Recommendation

It's great to receive messages from those receiving from the ministry. This will expose supporters to the impact of the ministry that is happening.

Remember that as ministry partners your supporters are sharing in making this happen, so it makes sense to give some feedback on the ministry. This will only further your work and give assurance to your supporters that their financial support is being invested correctly. They may be encouraged about the harvest that is happening and they may tell their friends who have a similar heart for your ministry or may wish to increase their financial support in the future to help develop the ministry.

If your readers engage best with your emails, try to break up the text into paragraphs and short and longer sentences to make it easy to read, with a maximum of 5 lines or so. Adding relevant images with the text makes it more engaging and more effective.

Be Proactive in Adding New People To Your Email List

Building an email list is very important to developing your support base. Add people onto your email list as often as you can. They include those that are potential supporters too, who might have expressed an interest in your ministry. A simple message like this below is an effective method of adding people to your email list.

> *"If you would like to learn more about my ministry*
> *and would like to receive regular newsletters, please*
> *send me your email address. Thank you."*

Timing is also important. Asking them to join should be at times when your ministry has been highlighted to them and fresh in their minds, perhaps after a church meeting or in a discussion with friends. Make it as easy as possible for them.

As previously mentioned, ask your ministry partners if they would share with their friends that might be interested in hearing about your ministry. Kindly challenge them to ask five of their friends to help develop your ministry influence.

Remember to review your email list and delete any contacts that have asked to be removed, or contacts that you know are not opening the emails and you know are not interested in you and your ministry. Once you have done this you can see how many potential and current ministry partners you have in contact with at that time.

Check those people who you would think would be very interested in your ministry but haven't opened an email in a long time as they may well not use that email address anymore. Seasons also come and go and people might be with you and your ministry for one season or for the rest of your life.

On Facebook send out invitations to others to receive your newsletter after every significant news or ministry event has happened that has generated a lot of interest. Also, send an invitation on Facebook every 3 months to generally remind people.

When To Send Your Email

MailChimp gives you the Open Rates (%) for your emails, which is very useful information. Send emails at different times and days to test. Saturday morning around 9:00am is a good time as it provides the weekend for people to read your news and respond to anything you are asking them to do, like asking for support.

"So do not worry, saying, 'What shall we eat?' or 'What shall we drink?' For the pagans run after all these things, and your heavenly Father knows that you need them."

Matthew 6:31-32

EASY ACTION
#10

Supercharge
Your Social Media

Social Media is part of the daily routine for a lot of people, including your supporters. Facebook, Twitter, Instagram are amongst the most popular channels in the social media world and supporters may wish to receive contact through these channels. For example, for using Facebook the option of setting up a *Group* is a great way to create a gated community where you can post updates. Privacy settings can also be changed for only the people you have invited will be able to view the content. You can then share on your own profile as well.

Find Where Your Supporters Are

Whatever your preferences are, use the channels preferred by each individual supporter where possible. There's not much value trying to communicate on a channel that a person is not using or is not keen on. As with email and all forms of communication, try your best to ensure that what you are communicating gets through to your intended audience.

Be Consistent

A very important rule is to be consistent with your social media content. People are creatures of habit and love a bit of routine. As in any relationship, regular contact is a defining attribute. The most important aspect of communication is to keep active and consistent with good quality content. With social media you can post lots of things, such as messages, images and videos.

To help in being consistent scheduling posts and tweets in advance is a tool I would highly recommend if you have a Facebook page or a Twitter account. Make the most of these different forms of communication but ensure that the content is relevant and interesting to your audience.

Video Content

For publishing videos the best performing videos are usually around 1 minute, as many people's attention spans do not last that long. However, if you have a story that draws in the viewer, this can stretch their attention longer between 2 to 10 minutes for most instances. A good example of a video would be to share a recent story with a backdrop that is relevant to your story. Perhaps you work in a medical centre. You could have someone hold your phone whilst you record a story with the medical centre in the background. Practice your video making and get a friend or two to give you some feedback.

New Initiatives and Best Practice
Ask fellow ministry workers how they use social media and what new social media channels or tools they finding beneficial. As you share best practice you might find some new exciting ways to communicate your ministry and gain new audiences as a result. There are always plenty of training courses available that can often be found online for free or a small amount.

Remember that not everyone uses the same social media channels, so keep it in mind and post the same content on all of your channels as much as you can.

"If any of you lacks wisdom, you should ask God, who gives generously to all without finding fault, and it will be given to you."

James 1:5

EASY
ACTION
#11

Improve
Your Giving

Find ways of how to bless your supporters. Here are some ideas on how to give:

- Postcards on Outreach
- Postcards on Sabbatical
- Gifts from Ministry Area
- Products from Ministries
- Spend Time with Supporters
- Take Part in Ministry on Your Visit
- Invitation to Visit Ministry Location

Remember, ministry supporters are generally busy in their own lives, working a full time job or responsibility. They need to rest up when they are on holiday, so try to help them in this while sharing with the ministry.

Perhaps they wish to visit - if so make it easy for them to visit. Say that you have time in a month in the future where you could both catch up and suggest hosting them for a holiday (make sure that they agree it would be a holiday for them too!). Here are a few examples of what a missionary could say:

> *"We can take you on a tour of Oxford if you would like?"*
> *"We have friends that you can stay with."*
> *"We would recommend these Airbnb places..."*

Make it easy and try one of these ideas at a time and see how it goes. Make a list of people that you're thinking of and write them down on the next page. Remember, this applies to potential supporters as well. On the next page list your supporters and go through the ideas highlighted. Add a date when you could possibly do this and any other relevant information.

Date	Name of Supporter	How can I bless them?
1		
2		
3		
4		
5		
6		
7		
8		
9		
10		
11		
12		
13		
14		
15		

The Ministry Fridge Magnet

Supporters will, very likely, appreciate a nicely designed, quality fridge magnet to put on their fridge. Don't underestimate the fridge magnet. It will be seen by your supporters in their kitchens and will serve as a daily reminder of their partnership in your ministry. Use a great quality picture with yourself smiling, your ministry in the background and your details (e.g. Chris in Uganda) with a thank you message to your supporters (include their names to make it personal) and you'll add joy to their day. Another suggestion is to create an annual customized ministry calendar to put on the wall.

*"And my God will meet all your needs according to
the riches of his glory in Christ Jesus."*

Philippians 4:19

EASY
ACTION
#12

Improve
Your Receiving

Finally, make it as quick and easy as possible to receive finances from your current supporters. This also applies to new supporters that wish to start financial giving to your ministry.

Your new supporter may never have supported a missionary before, so the whole process will be brand new to them. They may lead busy lives and may not be able to dedicate valuable time to the process of figuring out how to give. Helping them by making it easy would be a great help.

Be quick to respond to new supporters who wish to give. Even if you can't fully respond to the new supporters at the time, send a message acknowledging the message and letting them know if you are thankful and that you will be in touch at a certain point in the near future (such as the weekend or day when you are free).

For financial giving, providing options for receiving finances gives people a choice that they may prefer. Keeping in touch with your supporters on a consistent basis helps to provide opportunities for your supporters to give to your ministry, whether it is financially, prayer support or another.

Those that want to give to you will welcome the process being as straightforward as possible. Do everything you can to ensure that your ability to receive from your supporters is as effective as your ability to give.

"For I am the LORD your God who takes hold of your right hand and says to you, Do not fear; I will help you."

Isaiah 41:13

Acknowledgments

Thank you God for this opportunity to bless others in their ministries. Thank you to the Nunn family, Rick and Sue Joyce, Laura Bridges, Sean and Fay Older, Sally Raynham, Laura M for your valuable help in making this book happen.

Add Your Review

If this book was helpful to you please leave a review on Amazon.

Notes

Notes

Notes

Notes

Printed in Great Britain
by Amazon

79186547R00048